DEALING WITH ANGER PROBLEMS:
RATIONAL-EMOTIVE
THERAPEUTIC INTERVENTIONS

Windy Dryden, PhD
Goldsmith's College
University of London

Professional Resource Exchange, Inc.
Sarasota, Florida

Paperbound Edition ISBN: 0-943158-59-1
Library of Congress Catalog Card Number: 90-52986

The copy editor for this book was Patricia Hammond, the
managing editor was Debbie Fink, the graphics coordina-
tor was Laurie Girsch, and the cover designer was Bill
Tabler.

PRACTITIONER'S RESOURCE SERIES

Dealing with Anger Problems

Peter A. Keller, PhD
Chair, Department of Psychology
Mansfield University
Mansfield, Pennsylvania

R. John Wakeman, PhD
Head, Department of Clinical Psychology
Ochsner Clinic and Ochsner Foundation Hospital
New Orleans, Louisiana

SERIES PREFACE

As a publisher of books, cassettes, and continuing education programs, the Professional Resource Exchange strives to provide mental health professionals with highly applied resources that can be used to enhance clinical skills and expand practical knowledge.

All of the titles in the *Practitioner's Resource Series* are designed to provide important new information on topics of vital concern to psychologists, clinical social workers, marriage and family therapists, psychiatrists, and other mental health professionals.

Although the focus and content of each book in this series will be quite different, there will be notable similarities:

1. Each title in the series will address a timely topic of critical clinical importance.

2. The target audience for each title will be practicing mental health professionals. Our authors were chosen for their ability to provide concrete "how-to-do-it" guidance to colleagues who are trying to increase their competence in dealing with complex clinical problems.

3. The information provided in these books will represent "state-of-the-art" information and techniques derived from both clinical experience and empirical research. Each of these guide books will include references and resources for those who wish to pursue more advanced study of the discussed topic.

4. The authors will provide numerous case studies, specific recommendations for practice, and the types of "nitty-gritty" details that clinicians need before they can incorporate new concepts and procedures into their practices.

We feel that one of the unique assets of the Professional Resource Exchange is that all of its editorial decisions are made by mental health professionals. The publisher, Larry Ritt, is a clinical psychologist and marriage and family therapist who maintains an active independent practice. The senior editor, Peter Keller, is a clinical psychologist who currently serves as chair of a psychology department and is actively involved in clinical training.

The editor of this series, Hal Smith, is a clinical psychologist in independent practice. He holds a diplomate in clinical psychology from the American Board of Professional Psychology, a diplomate in forensic psychology from the American Board of Forensic Psychology, and a diplomate in clinical neuropsychology from the American Board of Professional Neuropsychology. His specialties include clinical and forensic psychology, neuropsychology, stress management, management of chronic pain and psychophysiologic disorders, learning disabilities, interventions for spouse abusers, psychotherapy, psychodiagnostic evaluations, clinical hypnosis, and consultation.

We are also fortunate to have the services of an exceptionally well-qualified panel of consulting editors who assist in the selection and preparation of titles for this series: William D. Anton, Judith V. Becker, Philip C. Boswell, Florence Kaslow, and R. John Wakeman. Our consulting editors are all highly experienced clinicians. In addition, they have all made significant contributions to their professions as scholars, teachers, workshop leaders, researchers, and/or as authors and editors.

Lawrence G. Ritt, Publisher
Harold H. Smith, Jr., Series Editor

FOREWORD

Windy Dryden has recently authored more than 20 books on psychotherapy and has become one of the foremost writers on rational-emotive therapy (RET). The present book, *Dealing with Anger Problems: Rational-Emotive Therapeutic Interventions*, is one of his very best. It updates my earlier book, *Anger--How to Live With and Without It* (Ellis, 1977) and provides a down-to-earth, hard-headed, succinct guidebook on the use of RET with a wide variety of common anger and aggression problems.

As Dr. Dryden shows, anger is a highly important, and potentially very disruptive, part of human life. It not only creates many personal and interpersonal problems, but it also has serious societal and global consequences, particularly in an age of nuclear fission and atomic warheads (Ellis, 1986, 1990; Ellis & Yeager, 1989). Unless therapists, educators, and others do something effective to help people curb their angry outbursts, who knows how long the human race will be around to work at coping with hostility.

Dealing with Anger Problems is the most effective book I have read in this area for several reasons:

1. It briefly and accurately presents the basic theory and practice of RET and makes it marvelously clear and understandable to any open-minded therapist.
2. It concretely applies RET to many varieties of anger and many common situations in which it is likely to occur.

3. It includes actual dialogues between clients and the author, which show just how RET can be done; and it stops the tape from time to time to indicate exactly why certain interventions are made.
4. It precisely outlines and fills in the specific therapeutic steps that can be efficiently taken by an RET practitioner working with typical angry clients.

The rational-emotive and cognitive-behavior approach to assessing and treating anger problems is no panacea and has distinct limitations with some clients some of the time. But it has now been partially validated not only by many case histories but, more scientifically, by a score of controlled outcome studies. Now that Windy Dryden has succinctly presented RET anger control techniques in this book, I think that his clearcut methods will lead to many more successful cases and outcome studies.

REFERENCES

Ellis, A. (1977). *Anger--How to Live With and Without It.* Secaucus, NJ: Citadel Press.

Ellis, A. (1986). Fanaticism that may lead to a nuclear holocaust: The contributions of scientific counseling and psychotherapy. *Journal of Counseling and Development, 65,* 146-151.

Ellis, A. (1990, August). *The Contributions of Psychotherapy to Achieving Peace: The Rational-Emotive Approach.* Paper delivered at the Annual Convention of the American Psychological Association, Boston, MA.

Ellis, A., & Yeager, R. (1989). *Why Some Therapies Don't Work: The Dangers of Transpersonal Psychology.* Buffalo, NY: Prometheus.

Albert Ellis, PhD
President
Institute for Rational-Emotive Therapy
45 East 65th Street
New York, NY   10021

ABSTRACT

This short guide considers the rational-emotive approach to dealing with clients' anger problems. First, I will introduce the basic principles of rational-emotive theory. Second, I will outline how rational-emotive therapists conceptualize clients' anger problems. Finally, I will present the 12 steps of the rational-emotive treatment sequence when dealing with clients' anger problems, illustrating these steps with verbatim excerpts from an actual case.

TABLE OF CONTENTS

CONCEPTUALIZING ANGER PROBLEMS *(Continued)*

THE RATIONAL-EMOTIVE TREATMENT SEQUENCE

THE RATIONAL-EMOTIVE
TREATMENT SEQUENCE *(Continued)*

DEALING WITH ANGER PROBLEMS: RATIONAL-EMOTIVE THERAPEUTIC INTERVENTIONS

BASIC PRINCIPLES OF RATIONAL-EMOTIVE THEORY

In this section, I will outline some basic principles of rational-emotive theory. First, I will place rational-emotive therapy (RET) in its historical context. Second, I will consider the meaning of the terms rationality and irrationality in the context of human goals and purposes. Third, I will discuss how RET advocates the principles of responsible hedonism and enlightened self-interest. Fourth, I will describe RET's philosophic and scientific emphasis and humanistic outlook. Fifth, I will discuss RET's well-known ABC framework. Sixth, I will put forward two basic biological tendencies which are relevant to the theory and practice of RET. Finally, I will outline briefly the RET theory of change.

HISTORICAL CONTEXT

Rational-emotive therapy was originated in 1955 by Albert Ellis, a New York clinical psychologist. Ellis originally worked as a psychoanalyst, but although he enjoyed practicing this mode of therapy, he later became dissatisfied with it because it was, in his words, "inefficient," in that it took a long time and did not produce very effective therapeutic results. For a while Ellis experimented with the shorter-term psychoanalytic psychotherapy and with various eclectic approaches. He then founded RET. In doing so, he was influenced more by philosophers than

1

by psychologists, returning to a longstanding interest he had had in practical approaches within the philosophic tradition. In particular, he was influenced by the views of Epictetus, a Roman philosopher, who stated that "men are disturbed not by things but by their view of things."

In the mid 1950s most therapists were influenced by psychoanalytic theories and methods; thus, to emphasize the logical and cognitive disputing aspects of his therapeutic approach, Ellis called his method "rational therapy." This caused problems because it was generally assumed that rational therapy only involved a focus on cognition (i.e., thoughts and beliefs). From the beginning, however, Ellis held that cognition, emotion, and behavior were inter-related psychological processes and that his approach to therapy emphasized all three. To counter unwarranted criticisms of rational therapy, specifically that it neglected emotion, Ellis in 1961 renamed his approach "rational-emotive therapy." To further make the point, Ellis titled his first major book on RET *Reason and Emotion in Psychotherapy* (Ellis, 1962). Although the name rational-emotive therapy has remained unchanged to this day, Ellis has argued that his approach could easily have been called rational-emotive-behavior therapy because in addition to focusing on clients' emotions and beliefs, rational-emotive therapists encourage their clients to actively put into practice what they learn in therapy through the use of behavioral methods.

GOALS, PURPOSES, AND RATIONALITY

According to rational-emotive theory, we humans are happiest when we set up important life goals and purposes and actively strive to achieve them. In the process, we acknowledge that we live in a social world, and thus we are encouraged to develop a philosophy of enlightened self-interest. This involves pursuing our valued goals while demonstrating what Alfred Adler called "social interest" - a commitment both to helping others achieve their valued goals and to making the world a socially and environmentally better place in which to live.

Given that we tend to be goal directed, *rational* in RET theory means "that which helps people to achieve their basic goals and purposes, whereas irrational means that which prevents them from achieving these goals and purposes" (Dryden, 1984, p. 238). While rationality is not defined in any absolute sense, it contains three major

2

criteria: pragmatism, logic, and a basis in reality. Thus a more extended definition of rationality would be (a) that which helps people to achieve their basic goals and purposes; (b) that which is logical (nonabsolutist); and (c) that which is empirically consistent with reality. Conversely, an extended definition of irrationality would be (a) that which prevents people from achieving their basic goals and purposes; (b) that which is illogical (especially, dogmatic and musturbatory); and (c) that which is empirically inconsistent with reality.

RESPONSIBLE HEDONISM

Rational-emotive theory argues that, as humans, we are basically hedonistic in the sense that we seek to stay alive and to achieve a reasonable degree of happiness. Here hedonism does not mean "the pleasures of the flesh" but involves the concept of personal meaning. A person is said to be acting hedonistically when he or she is happy acting in a way that is personally meaningful. The concept of responsible hedonism means that we are mindful of the fact that we live in a social world and that, ideally, our personally meaningful actions should help make the world a better place in which to live or, at the very least, not unduly harm anyone.

Rational-emotive theory makes an important distinction between short-range and long-range hedonism. We are likely to be at our happiest when we succeed in achieving both our short-term and our long-term goals. Frequently, however, we defeat ourselves by attempting to satisfy our short-term goals and, in the process, sabotage our long-term goals. For example, we often strive to avoid immediate discomfort when it would be better for us to experience that discomfort because doing so would help to achieve our long-term goals. Rational-emotive therapists encourage their clients to achieve a balance between the pursuit of their short- and long-range goals, while recognizing that what represents a healthy balance for a given person is best judged by that person.

ENLIGHTENED SELF-INTEREST

Rational-emotive therapists have often been accused of advocating selfishness because they encourage their clients in the pursuit of happiness. However, this is not so if selfishness is defined as "the ruthless pursuit of one's goals while cynically disregarding the goals and view-points of others." Rather, rational-emotive therapists encourage their clients to demonstrate enlightened self-interest, which involves putting themselves first most of the time while putting others, and particularly significant others, a close second. Enlightened self-interest can also involve putting the desires of others before our own, particularly when the welfare and happiness of those others are of great importance to them and our desires are not primary. Self-sacrifice is discouraged unless the person wants to sacrifice himself or herself and finds personal meaning and happiness in doing so.

PHILOSOPHIC AND SCIENTIFIC EMPHASIS

Rational-emotive theory stresses that we are born philosophers. We have the ability to think about our thinking and to realize that we are highly influenced by our implicit philosophies of life which are either flexible and undogmatic or musturbatory and absolutist. Rational-emotive theory agrees with the ideas of George Kelly (1955) that we are also scientists and are able to appreciate that our philosophies are basically hypotheses about ourselves, other people, and the world which need to be tested. This is best done using our philosophical abilities, particularly our ability to think critically about the logical and illogical aspects of our thought.

Ellis (1976) has argued that humans have a strong tendency to think and act irrationally. We also have the ability to think critically about our thinking and behavior; to correct the illogicalities in our thinking; and to judge whether or not our hypotheses are consistent with reality. Rational-emotive theorists do, however, recognize that reality cannot be judged in any absolute manner but is best regarded as accurate if it is seen as such by a group of neutral observers (the principle of consensual reality).

HUMANISTIC OUTLOOK

RET is not only philosophical and scientific in orientation but takes a specific humanistic-existential approach to human problems and their solutions. This view conceptualizes humans as holistic, indivisible, goal-directed organisms who have importance in the world just because we are human and alive. It encourages us to unconditionally accept ourselves with our limitations but, at the same time, work toward minimizing our limitations. RET agrees with the position of ethical humanism which "encourages people to live by rules emphasizing human interests over the interests of inanimate nature, of lower animals or of any assumed natural order or deity" (Ellis, 1980, p. 327). However, this does not mean being ecologically and environmentally insensitive, advocating the mindless slaughter of animals, or being disrespectful of others' religious views. Furthermore, this outlook acknowledges that we are human and in no way superhuman or subhuman.

THE ABC FRAMEWORK

The ABC framework is the cornerstone of RET practice and therefore it merits detailed attention. "A" stands for an activating event which may be external or internal to your client. When A refers to an external event, then it can be said that the event actually occurred if your client's descriptions of it can be confirmed as accurate by neutral observers (the principle of consensual reality). But here A will also stand for your client's inference (or interpretation) about the event.

"B" stands for beliefs. These are evaluative cognitions (or thoughts) which are either rigid or flexible. When these beliefs are rigid they are called *irrational beliefs* and take the form of musts, absolute shoulds, have to's, got to's, and so on. When your client adheres to such rigid beliefs, he will tend to make irrational conclusions from these irrational premises.* These irrational conclusions take the form of (a) *awfulizing* - meaning more than 100% bad, worse than it absolutely should be; (b) *I-can't-stand-it-itis* (or low frustration tolerance) - meaning that your client cannot envision having any happiness at all if what he demands must not exist actually does exist; and (c) *damnation* - meaning your client will damn himself, other people, and/or life conditions.

When your client's beliefs are flexible they are called *rational beliefs* in RET. Flexible beliefs often take the form of desires, wishes, wants, and preferences which your client does not escalate into dogmatic musts, shoulds,

---

*In this guide the client will be male and the therapist, female. This usage was determined by a toss of a coin.

oughts, and so on. When your client adheres to such flexible rational beliefs he will tend to make rational conclusions from these rational premises. These conclusions take the form of (a) *evaluations of badness* - here, for example, your client will conclude "It's bad, but not terrible" rather than "It's awful" when faced with a negative activating event; (b) *statements of toleration* - here your client may say "I don't like it, but I can bear it"; and (c) *acceptance of fallibility* - here your client will accept himself and other people as fallible human beings who cannot legitimately be given a single global rating. Also, your client will accept the world and life conditions as complex, composed of good, bad, and neutral elements, and thus will also refrain from giving the world a global rating.

"C" in the ABC framework stands for emotional and behavioral consequences of your client's beliefs about A. In RET, the C's that follow from irrational, rigid beliefs about negative A's are called *inappropriate* negative consequences, and C's that follow from rational flexible beliefs about negative A's are termed *appropriate* negative consequences.

The focus of this guide is on anger problems. In rational-emotive theory, the term "anger" is used to refer to an inappropriate negative emotion that stems from irrational beliefs; the term "annoyance" is used to refer to an appropriate negative emotion that stems from rational beliefs.

Three Basic Musts. While your clients will often express their irrational beliefs in personally distinctive terms, you might find it helpful to consider these individualistic beliefs as variations of the three basic musts:

Basic Must #1: Demands About Self. The first basic must concerns your client's demands about himself and is often stated in these terms: "I must do well and be approved by significant others and if I'm not, then it is awful. I can't stand it, and I am a damnable person to some degree when I am not loved or when I do not do well." These beliefs often lead to anxiety, depression, shame, and guilt. Anger often serves to protect your client from threats to his self-worth.

Must #2: Demands About Others. The second basic must concerns your client's demands about other people, and is often expressed as follows: "You must treat me well and justly, and it's awful and I can't bear it when you don't. You are damnable when you don't treat me well and you deserve to be punished for doing what you must not do." Such beliefs are often associated with feelings of anger, passive-aggressive behavior, and acts of violence.

Basic Must #3: Demands About the World/Life Conditions. The third basic must concerns your client's demands about the world or life conditions and often takes the following form: "Life conditions under which I live absolutely must be the way I want them to be and, if they are not, it's terrible, I can't stand it, poor me." This belief is associated with feelings of "hurt anger" and sulking behavior. Your client may also have problems of self-discipline such as procrastination and addictions which serve to protect him from his hurt and angry feelings.

A, B, and C Interact. As I have presented the ABC framework, it states that A (activating events and/or inferences of these events) activates your client's evaluative beliefs (B) which leads to feelings and behavior at C. However, this is oversimplified; in reality, A, B, and C frequently interact. For example, your client's dogmatic beliefs at B will often lead him to make overly negative inferences at A, or to focus on particular features of A which he might not attend to if he had rational beliefs. Thus, if your client dogmatically believes that he must not be rejected socially, he may overestimate the likelihood of being rejected and may focus on the negative statements that others make about him to the exclusion of neutral or positive statements. In addition, when your client is experiencing anger, for example, this feeling (C) may lead him to evaluate (B) events in an overly hostile way. Furthermore, when your client is in a situation at A, being in that context may influence him to make certain evaluations (B) that he might not make in other situations. Thus, if your client was treated unfairly, he might be more likely to hold anger-creating beliefs than if he was treated in a just manner. Although A, B, and C often interact in quite complex ways (Ellis, 1985a), in this guide I will restrict myself to the simplified ABC framework.

TWO BASIC BIOLOGICAL HUMAN TENDENCIES

Albert Ellis (1976) has made the important point that humans very easily tend to escalate their desires (particularly when those desires are strong) into absolute musts. The fact that we seem to do this so easily, and to such a great extent, has led Ellis to conclude that this constitutes a basic biological tendency of most, if not all, humans (see Ellis, 1976, for a more detailed exposition of this argument). While Ellis does acknowledge that social influences also have an effect in this regard, he has noted that "Even if everybody had had the most rational upbringing, virtually all humans would often irrationally escalate their individual and social preferences into absolute demands on (a) themselves, (b) other people, and (c) the universe around them" (Ellis, 1984a, p. 20). However, Ellis also stresses that humans have a second basic biological tendency which allows them to exercise the power of choice and to identify, challenge, and change their irrational thinking. So, although we seem to have a strong biological tendency to think irrationally, we are not seen as slaves to this tendency and can work to overcome it (although not fully so) by repeatedly striving to change our irrational beliefs.

THEORY OF CHANGE

Given that we are not slaves to our tendency to think irrationally, RET argues that we can change, particularly if we internalize three major insights:

Insight #1. Past or present activating events do not "cause" your client's disturbed emotional and behavioral consequences. Rather it is his belief system about these activating events that "creates" his disturbed feelings and behaviors.

Insight #2. Irrespective of how your client disturbed himself in the past, he *now* upsets himself largely because he keeps re-indoctrinating himself with his irrational beliefs.

Insight #3. Because your client is human and he very easily and, to some degree, naturally tends to disturb himself, and because he finds it easy to cling to his self-defeating thoughts, feelings, and actions, he can only overcome his disturbances by working hard and repeatedly both to dispute his irrational beliefs and to counteract the effects of these beliefs.

Having outlined the basic principles of rational-emotive theory, I will now consider how rational-emotive therapists conceptualize their clients' anger problems.

CONCEPTUALIZING ANGER PROBLEMS

I wish first to outline a number of points:

1. Many words are commonly used to describe anger: rage, resentment, hate, hostility, and so on. In this guide I will use the term anger throughout, because in RET the irrational beliefs that underpin anger are considered to be the same as those that underpin these other terms.
2. I will not focus here on clinical problems where physical violence is an integral component of a person's anger, because this topic alone warrants a separate book if it is to be covered comprehensively.
3. As noted in the previous section, in rational-emotive theory anger is considered to be an inappropriate negative emotion because it stems from a person's irrational beliefs. Conversely, annoyance is considered to be an appropriate negative emotion in that it stems from a person's rational beliefs. Please keep this distinction firmly in mind throughout this guide because it is at the core of the rational-emotive approach to treating anger problems.

I will now distinguish between three objects of a person's anger - (a) anger at others, (b) anger at impersonal objects and life conditions, and (c) anger at self - and consider how RET therapists conceptualize each.

ANGER AT OTHERS

A number of cognitive-behavioral therapists (e.g., Beck, 1976; Ellis, 1977a; Grieger, 1982; Howells, 1988) have noted that when people make themselves angry at other people, the triggering activating events or inferences about these events (at A in the ABC framework) involve four major themes. These themes represent situations when other people (a) frustrate or block the client in pursuit of his goals; (b) directly attack the client or what he values; (c) are deemed to threaten the client or what he values; and (d) transgress the client's rules.

In this section I will deal with each of these triggers separately. I will outline both the irrational beliefs that underpin each type of interpersonal anger and the rational beliefs that underlie the more appropriate emotional response to these triggers (i.e., annoyance). Case vignettes will be used to illustrate the points made.

Frustration. Clients who often make themselves angry when other people frustrate them in pursuit of their goals do so for two major reasons: (a) They have a philosophy of low frustration tolerance (LFT), and/or (b) they are blocked from achieving something to which they have attached their self-worth.

Case Vignette 1: LFT Anger in Response to Frustration. John frequently made himself angry whenever anybody got in his way (e.g., when he was driving, when other people were standing in line in front of him, whenever anybody kept him waiting). He made himself angry because (a) he demanded that he *must not* be frustrated; (b) he evaluated being frustrated as *awful*, something (c) that he *could not stand*; and (d) he rated other people who frustrated him as *damnable*.

The therapeutic task with John is to help him raise his level of frustration tolerance. His RET therapist will endeavor to help him to believe that (a) frustration is undesirable but that there is no law of the universe that states that he must not be frustrated; (b) frustration is an inconvenience, not a horror; (c) he can tolerate being frustrated without ever liking it; and (d) others are fallible human beings who have their own agendas and will often frustrate him in pursuit of their goals. Once John has begun to internalize these rational beliefs he will be annoyed at being frustrated but will not make himself self-defeatingly angry whenever anybody gets in his way.

Case Vignette 2: Self-Worth Anger in Response to Frustration. Joan, an executive secretary, had set her heart on gaining promotion at work. However, one of her friends got the job. Joan responded to this obstacle to reaching her valued goal with anger at her friend and at the appointments committee which failed to offer her the job. Joan made herself angry because she had attached her self-worth to achieving promotion. Her major irrational belief was "I *must* achieve that which is very important to me and I'm *no good* if I don't." Consequently, she regarded her failure as *awful,* something that was *unbearable,* and she viewed others as *rotten* (a) for preventing her from achieving something that she believed she had to achieve and (b) for exposing her to her own sense of inadequacy as a person. Here, as elsewhere, self-worth anger is partially an attempt to place the blame on others rather than on one's self.

In order to help Joan experience healthy annoyance (as well as sadness and disappointment) instead of self-defeating anger (and depression), her RET therapist will strive to convince her that it would have been highly desirable for her to achieve her valued goal but not necessary for her to do so, and that she can accept herself as a fallible human being (FHB) who had failed rather than as a complete failure. Having done this, it becomes easier to help her see that (a) failure is bad but not awful, (b) that she can stand what she believed she could not, and (c) that her friend and the members of the appointments committee are also fallible human beings who have a right to act according to their own set of values.

Direct Attack. Clients who make themselves angry when other people attack them or what they value, do so because they have a philosophy of LFT and/or they seek to preserve their self-worth.

Case Vignette 3: LFT Anger in Response to Direct Attack. Harry made himself angry when his friend's 11-year-old son accidentally broke one of his valuable vases. He did so primarily because he believed that he *must not* lose (or have destroyed) that which he valued. Consequently he believed that (a) it was *awful* that the boy broke his vase, (b) that he *couldn't stand* to lose what was important to him, and (c) that the boy himself was *no good* for being so careless. Note, however, that Harry did not attach his self-worth to his vase and thus did not make himself angry to protect his self-esteem.

In order to feel annoyed rather than angry in this episode, Harry would have had to believe that it would be highly desirable for him to retain that which he strongly values but that there is no reason to support his claim that he absolutely has to. Then it would be easier for him to acknowledge that his loss was (a) bad (but not awful); (b) something that could be accepted as having happened (but not liked); and (c) that while the boy's carelessness was bad, he was a fallible youngster who would frequently do the wrong thing. In this annoyed frame of mind Harry could reasonably negotiate compensation from his friend, something he would be less likely to do successfully if he were angry.

Case Vignette 4: Self-Worth Anger in Response to Direct Attack. Howie was arrested and charged with physical assault for punching his job supervisor on the nose. He did so when the supervisor called him "stupid, worthless, and useless" for failing to master quickly a new job procedure. During therapy, his RET counselor discovered that Howie responded so angrily in order to cover up his self-hatred. Howie admitted that under the surface he had been demanding that he *must* learn the new procedure quickly and that he would be stupid and worthless if he didn't. His supervisor's verbal attack had reminded him of his own inadequacy and, in an attempt to cover up these feelings, he physically attacked his attacker. His counselor also discovered that Howie considered that he *had to* hit his supervisor because, if he did not, his friends who had witnessed the incident would probably view him as a "weak, gutless slob" - an evaluation which, if made, he would then apply to himself.

Given these self-worth related irrational beliefs, Howie concluded that being attacked by his supervisor was (a) *terrible* and something that he (b) *could not tolerate*, and that (c) the supervisor was *damnable* for criticizing him and for making him feel small (or more accurately - reminding him of his own inadequacy).

Howie's counselor helped him to see how he could have handled the situation more appropriately by responding with feelings of annoyance. The counselor first helped Howie to believe that while it was important for him to do well and be approved, these were not necessities and that he could accept himself as a fallible person with his failures, and in the face of possible disapproval from others. Believing this would help Howie to conclude more rationally that (a) being attacked by his supervisor and disapproved of by his friends would be a major hassle but not an "end of the world" horror, (b) he could endure these hassles, and (c) his supervisor was not bad, but the supervisor's behavior on this occasion was.

Perceived Threat. Clients sometimes make themselves angry when they interpret the behavior of others as a threat to their sense of comfort (a term broadly defined in rational-emotive theory) and in situations where they demand comfort (LFT), or as a threat to their self-worth. Threat-related anger differs from attack-related anger because in threat a direct attack has not yet occurred but is deemed by the person concerned to be on the horizon. Beck (1976) has noted that in threat-related anger the person is not preoccupied with imminent danger. When the person is so preoccupied, it is more likely that he or she will experience anxiety. Rational-emotive theorists would concur with this view, although they would argue that anxiety is experienced when the person holds irrational beliefs about the danger.

Case Vignette 5: LFT Anger in Response to an Inferred Threat. Cindy made herself angry at her in-laws when they unexpectedly visited her on an evening that she had set aside as a quiet time with her husband, Bob. She had been looking forward to the evening and her irrational belief was "Not only do I want to have a quiet evening with Bob, but I *must* have it." Given this belief, she concluded that (a) her in-laws' interruption was *terrible*, (b) she *couldn't tolerate* their presence, and (c) they were selfish, *rotten people* for depriving her of what she believed she needed. As it transpired, they had only planned to stay for a few minutes, but in her angry frame of mind Cindy had imagined that they would be staying for the entire evening, and it was to this inferred threat that she responded.

If Cindy had thought rationally about this threat she would have (a) preferred to have an uninterrupted evening with her husband but would not have demanded that she get what she wanted; (b) evaluated the interruption as bad, but not terrible; (c) shown herself that she could stand not getting what she wanted; and (d) accepted her in-laws as fallible human beings who were doing the wrong thing. In this state of mind, Cindy may have questioned the validity of her inference that her in-laws planned to stay the entire evening rather than assuming that this was a fact. If her inference was correct, she probably could have asserted herself more effectively (e.g., by requesting that they visit on another evening) when annoyed than when angry.

Case Vignette 6: Self-Worth Anger in Response to an Inferred Threat. Wanda made herself angry at her boyfriend when she saw him talking light-heartedly with an attractive blonde woman at a party. She inferred that this meant he found the other woman attractive and wanted to go to bed with her which, if true, she would see as a threat to her self-worth.

Wanda's jealous anger stemmed mainly from her demand that her boyfriend *must not* find any other woman attractive; if he did, this would prove that she was unattractive and worthless. Given this irrational belief Wanda concluded that (a) it would be *terrible* if her boyfriend found another woman attractive, (b) she *could not put up* with such behavior, and that (c) he was a two-timing *son of a bitch* for acting that way. Wanda's irrational beliefs encouraged her to form such inferences as "He finds her more attractive than me" and "He wants to go to bed with her." According to rational-emotive theory, Wanda then assumes that these inferences are true and makes herself angry about these "facts."

When she discussed this incident with her RET therapist, he first encouraged her to assume that her inferences were true. Then he helped her acquire the following major rational belief that would lead her to be annoyed but not angry: "I don't want my boyfriend to find any other women attractive, and I certainly don't want him to make a pass at anybody else, but there is no reason why he must not do these things. If he does it, that doesn't prove I am worthless. I can accept myself if he does prefer this woman to me although I would be annoyed if that happened." From this major rational belief, she would make the following rational conclusions: (a) "I don't like his behavior but it is not terrible that he is acting in an undesirable manner"; (b) "I can stand his behavior, although I'll never like it"; and (c) "He's a fallible human being who is acting in an unfortunate manner." With these rational beliefs, Wanda would be in a better frame of mind to question the validity of her inferences about her boyfriend's feelings about and intentions toward the other woman based on the evidence available to her.

Transgression Against a Rule. The final theme found in anger at others occurs when others transgress a rule decreed important by the holder of that rule (Beck, 1976). The content of the rule may vary considerably among individuals, but it frequently involves the expectation that others will treat *one* with justice, fairness, and consideration. In addition, some people make themselves angry when they see that *other people* are being treated unjustly, unfairly, or inconsiderately. Another category of rules which, if violated, provide the trigger for a person's anger involve situations when other people encroach on what the person considers to be his or her "rights" (e.g., for autonomy, freedom of speech, freedom from prejudice, due treatment to which one feels entitled).

As in the three categories discussed previously, clients make themselves angry when others transgress their rules because they have a philosophy of LFT and/or the transgression activates beliefs centered on lowered self-esteem.

Case Vignette 7: LFT Anger in Response to a Transgressed Rule. Mary often sulks angrily when her husband treats her unfairly. Her rule which he transgresses on such occasions involves her anticipation that he will treat her with due consideration. Her major irrational belief on such occasions is "Since I treat him with consideration, he *must* reciprocate. I do not deserve his bad treatment and I must not get what I do not deserve." Mary describes her feelings as a combination of hurt and anger. This "hurt anger" in Mary's case does not involve self-devaluation but an attitude of "poor me." The irrational conclusions that Mary makes from this primary demand are (a) "It is *terrible* that he treats me in a manner I do not deserve," (b) "I *can't stand* to be treated in this way," and (c) "He is a *selfish bastard* for treating me this way." Her sulkiness is an indirect way of punishing her husband for his behavior and an attempt to make him feel guilty.

Mary sought therapy for her marital difficulties and was helped to change her irrational beliefs to the following rational beliefs: (a) "I very much want my husband to treat me fairly but he doesn't have to do so. Indeed, he has to act in the very way that he does act since he responds to what goes on in his mind and not to what goes on in mine"; (b) "It's bad but hardly terrible that he acts inconsiderately to me"; (c) "I'll never like his bad behavior but I can damn well stand it"; and (d) "He is not a selfish bastard for acting inconsiderately but rather a fallible human being who has a tendency to act selfishly at times." With this set of rational beliefs, Mary set out to inform her husband in a determined manner that she did not like his inconsiderateness. Her feelings of annoyance activated her to try to change the situation, whereas her old feelings of hurt and anger encouraged her to engage in sulky withdrawal.

Case Vignette 8: Self-Worth Anger in Response to a Transgressed Rule. William had worked hard to get to the top of his profession. However, he had always attached his self-worth to achievement. Now that he had reached his goal, he respected himself and expected others to show him the respect which he considered he now richly deserved. William made himself furiously angry whenever any of his subordinates violated this rule for respectful behavior and treated him with what he regarded as lack of respect.

William made himself angry because of his implicit irrational belief: "I *must* be treated with respect by my subordinates and if they show that they do not respect me that proves that I am unworthy of respect and am basically worthless." From this basic irrational belief, William made the following irrational conclusions: (a) "It's *terrible* that my subordinates don't treat me as well as they should," (b) "I *cannot bear it* when they show that they do not respect me," and (c) "They are *rotten people* for treating me disrespectfully and for reminding me of my basic worthlessness."

For William to overcome his fury and yet be rationally annoyed at what he considers to be the disrespectful behavior of his subordinates, he would have to adhere to the following rational beliefs: (a) "I want to be treated with respect, but others do not have to obey my rule. If they disrespect me that's unfortunate but I can accept myself as a fallible human being whether or not others respect me and whether or not I remain at the top of my profession"; (b) "It's bad but hardly terrible when my subordinates don't treat me as well as I want them to"; (c) "I can damn well stand their bad behavior although I'll never like it"; and (d) "My subordinates are not rotten people for treating me disrespectfully. They are fallible, unrateable human beings who are acting against my desires. Tough!"

With this set of rational beliefs William is in a better position than he would be, if angry, to question the validity of his inferences that his subordinates are treating him with lack of respect. If he still decides that their behavior is disrespectful, his feelings of undamning annoyance will encourage him to attempt to influence his subordinates in a constructive way. On the other hand, William's feelings of damning anger will make it more likely that he will abuse his subordinates. If he does this he will de-

crease his chances that he will have good respectful relationships with them in the future.

ANGER AT IMPERSONAL
OBJECTS AND LIFE CONDITIONS

In the previous section I have shown that anger at
other people is based on a philosophy of low frustration
tolerance and/or is an attempt to preserve one's self-worth
by attacking those who trigger one's attitude of self-rejec-
tion. Both these basic reasons for anger are present when
the focus of one's anger is on impersonal objects and life
conditions.

Case Vignette 9: LFT Anger at an Impersonal Object.
Fred came to therapy to curb what he called his "very
expensive temper." In the past year he had broken $7,000
worth of computers by throwing them on the floor when
they failed to work. Because he was self-employed, this
was an expense he could hardly afford. The irrational
beliefs that underpin Fred's anger center on intolerance of
frustration - a theme that predominates in LFT anger at
objects and life conditions. His basic irrational belief was
"Things *must* go smoothly for me." From this belief he
concluded the following: (a) "It is *terrible* when things
don't work," (b) "I *can't stand* being frustrated when things
go wrong," and (c) "The world is a *rotten place* for making
such unreliable objects."
Fred's therapist helped him to raise his level of frustration tolerance by encouraging him to develop a rational
philosophy toward frustration. Note that this philosophy
did lead Fred to feel annoyed when things went wrong,
but this was considered by both Fred and his therapist to
be a realistic response to an undesirable event. Fred's
rational philosophy comprised the following beliefs: (a) "I
wish that things would go smoothly for me but they often
don't and they don't have to"; (b) "It's a hassle when
things don't go well but hardly awful"; (c) "I can tolerate
frustration although it's hardly pleasant"; and (d) "Just
because objects don't work hardly proves that the world is
a rotten place. The world is a complex mix of good,
neutral, and bad. Tough! That's the way it is."

Case Vignette 10: Self-Worth Anger at Life Conditions.
Debbie considered that punctuality, both her own and
others, was essential. She prided herself on never having

been late for an appointment. She managed this by setting out well in advance for any given meeting. One day, as usual, she left home in very good time for an important meeting with her boss. On this occasion she got caught in a very heavy traffic jam due to bridge damage. At this point Debbie realized that for almost the first time in her life she would be late for an appointment; consequently she made herself furiously angry. She kicked the car, broke the side-view mirrors, and smashed the wind screen. Furthermore, she ranted and raged against the world.

Debbie's unusual behavior can be explained when we realize what being late meant to her. The irrational beliefs about being late centered on self-worth issues. Her major irrational belief was "I *must* never be late for any appointment; if I am that proves how worthless I am." From this belief she derived the following irrational conclusions: (a) "It's *awful* that life conditions are preventing me from arriving on time for my appointment"; (b) "I *can't bear* being late"; and (c) "Life conditions are *rotten* for stopping me in this way."

The key to Debbie handling this situation more rationally lies in her changing her major irrational belief to "I much prefer to be on time for all my important appointments, but there is no law of the universe that decrees that I must always be on time. If I'm late I can accept myself as a fallible human being whether or not I am responsible for my lateness." Having changed this belief, Debbie could more rationally conclude (a) "It's unfortunate but not awful that life conditions will sometimes prevent me from being punctual"; (b) "I don't like being late but I can bear it"; and (c) "This particular life condition is pretty bad, but life conditions in general are a complex mixture of good, bad, and neutral. I'd better accept that that's the way things are."

ANGER AT SELF

Clients often make themselves angry at themselves when they violate their own rules or standards and when they demand that they must not do so. Such violations may refer to acts of commission (when they break their own rule by doing something) or acts of omission (when they break their own rule by failing to do something). Self-anger resembles guilt in that both involve the person demanding that he or she must act (or must not act) in a certain way and damning "self" as a consequence of failing to live up to such demands. However, in guilt the rule that the person considers that he or she has broken pertains to that person's moral code, whereas in self-anger the rule generally lies outside of the moral domain.

Case Vignette 11: Self-Worth Anger at Transgressing One's Own Rule. Barbie found it helpful to discuss some of her personal problems with her friends. However, she considered that it was inappropriate to do so with her parents because they would worry unduly about her for weeks afterwards. And yet whenever she visited them she would break her own rule and tell them about her problems. She did this, it emerged later in therapy, because she believed that she needed other people to show concern for her and offer her support. After she broke her rule of appropriate behavior with her parents, Barbie would make herself very angry at herself. She did so because she believed irrationally that "I *absolutely must* not act inappropriately with my parents." From this primary belief she concluded (a) "It's *awful* that I use my parents in this way"; (b) "I *cannot stand* my bad behavior"; and (c) "I'm *worthless* when I act inappropriately."

Her therapist successfully helped Barbie to change her belief so that she accepted herself for breaking her own rule, but she still felt annoyed at the way she acted. Doing so helped her to address her compulsion to seek sympathy and support from others. Her new rational philosophy comprised the following beliefs: (a) "I want to act appropriately with my parents but there is no reason why I absolutely must do so. In fact there is a reason why I don't. I've learned that I discuss my problems with them because I believe I need their sympathy and support and I plan to overcome this need in therapy"; (b) "It's unfortunate that I discuss my problems with my parents since they worry about me. However, it's not terrible that I do so and I plan to stop soon"; (c) "I can stand acting inappropriately although I'll never like it"; and (d) "I'm not worthless when I act inappropriately. I'm a fallible human with a problem."

THE RATIONAL-EMOTIVE TREATMENT SEQUENCE

In this section I will outline the rational-emotive treatment sequence to be used when dealing with your client's anger problem. I will assume that you and your client have agreed that anger is in fact his target problem. First, I will provide an overview of the RET treatment sequence. Each step will then be outlined in detail and illustrated with verbatim material from an actual case.

AN OVERVIEW OF THE
RET TREATMENT SEQUENCE

RET is a problem-focused approach to psychotherapy. As such, I recommend that you adopt a problem-solving attitude at the outset. I will assume that you and your client have agreed that you will work together on his feelings of anger. Referring to the ABC framework outlined in the first section of this guide, your client's anger is C. Once you have agreed that your client's C is anger, discuss with your client the advantages and disadvantages of changing his feelings of anger to those of annoyance. This is an important step because clients are often ambivalent about changing their feelings of anger. Alternatively, you may carry out this step after you have assessed A, B, and C.

Assuming that you have both agreed to work toward changing his feelings of anger to those of annoyance, go on to assess a typical example of his anger problem. Because you already have C - feelings of anger - proceed to assess A, which, you will recall, stands for the activating event (or inference about the event) that served to trigger his irrational beliefs that underpinned his anger. Next, help your client to understand that A does not cause C because there is a missing step, namely that his disturbed angry feelings are largely determined by his irrational beliefs at B. At this stage (or earlier, if it is more appropriate), you may check whether your client also has a secondary emotional problem, that is, an emotional problem about his anger. If he does have a secondary emotional problem and particularly where it significantly interferes with his original problem, agree that this will now become the focus for discussion. You can carry out an assessment of this secondary problem using the ABC framework.

Whatever problem (primary or secondary) you are now assessing, and assuming that you have correctly assessed A and C and helped the client understand that it is B that largely determines C rather than A, you are now able to assess your client's irrational beliefs. While you are doing this, help your client discriminate keenly between his irrational and rational beliefs. The next step is to help your client understand the relationship between his inappropriate negative emotion(s) at C and his irrational beliefs at B. When the client has understood this connection and can see that in order to overcome his emotional problem at C he needs to change his irrational beliefs at B, you will be in a position to help the client dispute his irrational beliefs.

During the disputing process you may use pragmatic, logical, and empirical arguments. The purpose of disputing is to help the client understand why his irrational beliefs are self-defeating, illogical, and empirically inconsistent with reality, and why the alternative rational beliefs are self-enhancing, logical, and realistic. Once your client has understood this, you will be ready to encourage him to consider ways in which he can put his understanding into practice.

Once your client has learned that gaining conviction in the new rational beliefs involves practice, you can negotiate appropriate homework assignments with him. The purpose of homework assignments is to help your client translate his knowledge (intellectual insight) into conviction (emotional insight). It is very important for you to check on your client's experiences in carrying out homework assignments. In particular, it is important for you to trouble-shoot any obstacles to change that your client identifies.

When your client has shown some progress, encourage him to practice his new rational beliefs in different contexts using different cognitive, emotive, and behavioral techniques. In this way your client will be able to integrate his new rational beliefs into his emotional and behavioral repertoire.

I will now outline the 12 steps of the rational-emotive treatment sequence (see Table 1, page 22 for a summary) in dealing with anger problems. I will illustrate these steps with verbatim excerpts from an actual case (to preserve client confidentiality, identifying data have been altered, and for purposes of clarity, transcript material has been slightly edited). In presenting the 12 treatment steps I will assume that you and your client have already agreed that the client's target problem is anger.

TABLE 1: THE RATIONAL-EMOTIVE
TREATMENT SEQUENCE

It is assumed that you and your client have agreed that anger is his target problem.

STEP 1: Discuss Goals for Change

STEP 2: Ask for a Specific Example of Your Client's Anger Problem

STEP 3: Assess A

STEP 4: Determine Whether or Not Your Client Has a Secondary Emotional Problem (and Assess if Appropriate)

STEP 5: Teach the B-C Connection

STEP 6: Assess Irrational Belief (iB)

STEP 7: Connect iB and C

STEP 8: Dispute iB

STEP 9: Prepare Your Client to Deepen His Conviction in His Rational Beliefs

STEP 10: Encourage Your Client to Put His New Learning into Practice

STEP 11: Check Homework Assignments

STEP 12: Facilitate the Working-Through Process

A = Activating Event (and Inference)
B = Belief
iB = Irrational Belief
C = Emotion

STEP 1: DISCUSS GOALS FOR CHANGE

Even when you and your client have agreed to focus on anger as his target problem, realize that your client will very likely be ambivalent about changing his feelings of anger. It is important for you to discuss your client's goals for change. This can be done either at this point or after Step 3.

Your client may be reluctant to give up his anger for a variety of reasons (DiGiuseppe, 1988). First, he may not understand what constitutes a constructive alternative to anger. If so, help him understand the constructive aspects of annoyance (i.e., it aids effective action and tends to lead to improved interpersonal relationships through a nonblaming discussion of what is going on in those relationships) and the destructive aspects of anger (i.e., it inhibits effective action and tends to lead to deteriorating interpersonal relationships).

Second, your client may believe that he is *supposed* to feel and show anger and that showing anger is a sign of strength. In that case it is worthwhile devoting some time to challenging his view and offering a different view (i.e., that anger is a problem rather than a strength in that it has negative intrapersonal and interpersonal consequences).

Third, your client may believe that if he does not angrily tell someone else off, that other person may not understand that your client disapproves of the other's actions. Here you can discuss the greater advantages of unangry assertion.

Finally, your client may believe that anger has good consequences. For example, he may tell you how powerful he feels when he is angry, or how getting things out of his system in an angry way is good for him. Here it is important to help him distinguish between short-term and long-term consequences and to show him that the consequences that he lists are in all probability short-term; the longer-term consequences of anger are generally negative. Thus, although he may feel powerful at the moment when he is angry, he may later find himself feeling powerful all alone, because powerful displays of anger will tend to alienate other people. Also, research tends to show that cathartic displays of anger have long-term negative consequences for a person's physical and psychological health (Tavris, 1982).

In the case that follows, Bernie, with his wife's encouragement, has sought therapy because of frequent angry outbursts. In the first verbatim excerpt, the therapist engages him in a discussion of his goals for change.

Therapist: So why is anger a problem for you?
Client: Well, my wife certainly seems to think it is.
Therapist: And what's your view?
Client: Well, it certainly seems to get me into trouble.
Therapist: But you seem hesitant.

Client: Well I certainly get mad and I do tell people how I feel. But I do have the idea that it's wrong and harmful to bottle things up.

Therapist: So is it the case that you think that either you get mad and tell people off or that you bottle up your feelings?

Client: Yes, I guess so.

Therapist: Well there is another alternative, one which acknowledges that you have negative feelings when other people act in a way that you don't like, but one which gives you greater freedom about whether or not to express your feelings. It seems from what you say that when you get mad it's hard to control your feelings.

Client: You're right there.

Therapist: So would you be interested in that third alternative?

Client: Well I'd certainly like to know more.

Therapist: Well let's look at a specific example of your anger and I'll show you what I mean.

In this excerpt, as Bernie's therapist, I considered that he was genuinely interested in exploring the third alternative to which I alluded, but I thought that it was better for me to elaborate on this in the context of a specific example of his anger.

STEP 2: ASK FOR A SPECIFIC EXAMPLE OF YOUR CLIENT'S ANGER PROBLEM

To aid in the assessment of your client's anger problem, it is important for you to obtain a specific example. Your client experiences his anger and holds related irrational beliefs in *specific* contexts; therefore, being specific will help you obtain reliable and valid data about A, B, and C. It helps to give your client a plausible rationale for your specificity, especially if he tends to discuss his anger problem in vague terms. Help him understand that being specific about his problem will encourage him to deal more constructively with it in the situations about which he makes himself angry. A good way of modeling specificity for your client is for you to ask for a recent or a typical example of his anger problem.

Therapist: Well let's look at a specific example of your anger and I'll show you what I mean.

Client: What kind of example do you mean?

Therapist: Well one that gives me a clear example of what type of situation you typically make yourself angry about. It could be a recent example or one which you particularly remember.

STEP 3: ASSESS A

When you assess A, keep in mind that the activating event (or influence about this event) which triggered the irrational beliefs that underpin your client's anger is likely to involve (a) frustration, (b) direct attack, (c) threat, or (d) transgression of a rule.

It is important to note that irrational beliefs tend to lead to inferences that are negatively distorted (Ellis, 1977b). With respect to anger this means that your client may assume that when others frustrate him, directly attack him, threaten him, or transgress his rules, they (a) are unjustified in doing so; (b) do so intentionally; and (c) have malicious intent (Beck, 1976; Howells, 1988). You may be tempted to question the validity of this further set of inferences at this point. Resist this temptation. Rather, encourage your client to assume temporarily that A is correct. This will help you assess his irrational beliefs more accurately.

Identify the Part of A that Triggered B. While you are assessing A, help your client identify the most relevant part of A (i.e., the part of A that triggered your client's irrational belief at B). Because I include your client's inferences as part of A, it is important to recognize that his inferences are often chained (or linked together). Assess this chain with the purpose of identifying the most relevant link of the chain, that is, the aspect of A that triggered your client's irrational beliefs at B which, in turn, accounted for his angry feelings at C. You can do this by using a technique called inference chaining (Moore, 1988) - a procedure which helps you identify how your client's inferences are linked. I will include an example of inference chaining in the excerpt that follows:

Client: OK. I'll give you a recent typical example. We were at a dinner party with three other couples. Well, the other guys were sitting around talking about business and they all seemed to

be doing pretty well. One guy, Bill, was boast-
ing about how well he was doing. I could feel
myself getting quite tense. Well this guy, Bill,
started getting a bit big-headed and turned to
me, sort of sneered, and said "How are things
going at work for you, Bernie?" I was pretty
sure that he was trying to provoke me and I
got mad. I told him to shut his big mouth and
to mind his own business. Well, that really put
the cat among the pigeons. The other guys
looked at me as if I was mad and the women
got quite embarrassed. John, the host, eventu-
ally smoothed things over, but things were
pretty much uneasy for the rest of the night.

Therapist: So you made yourself mad about Bill's attempt
to provoke you, and the rest of the evening was
rather spoiled as a result.

[I attempt to pick the major theme from what Bernie has
said.]

Client: Yeah, that's right.

Therapist: Tell me, Bernie, let's assume for the moment
that you were right about Bill, that he was trying to provoke you. Provoke you in what way?

[I encourage Bernie to assume temporarily that his stated
inference about Bill's behavior is true (i.e., that Bill was
provoking him). Then I try to find out more about his
implicit inferences about the "provocation."]

Client: Well, I guess I thought he was trying to show
how great he was by showing me up to be a
chump.

Therapist: Why a chump?

Client: Because I'm not doing too well at work.

Therapist: And how do you feel about not doing too well
at work?

[I hypothesize that Bernie made himself angry because he
interpreted Bill's behavior as a threat to his personal
domain. If I am correct, then his anger served to protect
his personal domain from threat. I test out this hypothesis
by switching the inquiry to his feelings about his performance at work.]

Client: Not too good.
Therapist: How bad do you feel?
Client: Pretty shitty.
Therapist: I don't quite get the quality of the feeling.
Client: I feel depressed about it.

[I now have some evidence for my threat-anger hypothesis. To test it further I now deliberately change A to see how Bernie thought he would respond to a different event.]

Therapist: OK Bernie, that's something we'll explore further. But first I want to ask you two things. First, how do you think you would have felt about Bill's provocation if you were doing really well at work?
Client: Oh, I see . . . well let me think . . . I think I would have been pleased to have an opportunity to crow about how well I was doing.
Therapist: So you wouldn't have felt angry?
Client: No, I guess not.
Therapist: And, second, would you have felt angry about his provocation if you didn't feel shitty about not doing well at work?
Client: (Pause) That's a good question . . . no, I don't think I would . . . I think I can see what you're getting at. I still wouldn't like being reminded about not doing well but I would not have lost my cool in the way that I did.
Therapist: So there seems to be a relationship between you feeling depressed about your performance at work, Bill sort of touching on that issue, and your anger. What do you think?
Client: You've got a good case there, Doc.

[My threat-anger hypothesis can be confirmed. A is now "Being reminded about not doing well at work," C_1 is depression, and C_2 is anger serving to protect Bernie from Bill's threat. In Step 6, I will investigate what kind of irrational beliefs Bernie holds about the threat to produce C_1 and C_2. My hunch is that Bernie's irrational beliefs involve his self-worth.]

Avoid the Following Pitfalls while Assessing A. There are a number of pitfalls to avoid while assessing A. First, do not obtain too much detail about A. When your client does give you a lot of detail, try to abstract the salient theme from what he says, as I did with Bernie, or summarize what you understand to be the major aspect of A about which he may be emotionally disturbed. Allowing your client to talk at length about A will discourage you both from retaining a problem-solving approach to helping the client overcome his anger problem. If this happens, interrupt your client tactfully and re-establish a specific focus. For example, you could say to your client "I think you may be giving me more detail than I require; what was it about this situation that you were most angry about?"

Second, discourage your client from describing A in vague terms. Get as clear and as specific an example of A as you can.

In RET it is important for you to work on one A at a time. A third pitfall occurs when your client talks about several A's. If this happens, encourage your client to deal with the A which he considers to best illustrate the context in which he makes himself angry. Explain that you will deal with the other A's at a later date.

STEP 4: DETERMINE WHETHER OR NOT YOUR CLIENT HAS A SECONDARY EMOTIONAL PROBLEM (AND ASSESS IF APPROPRIATE)

Clients frequently have a variety of secondary emotional problems about their primary anger problem. It is important to assess whether or not your client has such a secondary problem. If your client's primary problem is anger you may ask "How do you feel about feeling angry?" to determine whether or not he does have a secondary emotional problem about his primary problem of anger. Frequent secondary problems about anger include guilt, shame (if anger is expressed in public), anxiety, and anger toward self for getting angry at others or life conditions.

When to Work on the Secondary Emotional Problem First. If your client does in fact have a secondary emotional problem, I suggest that you work on this problem first, under three conditions. First, if the existence of your client's secondary problem interferes significantly (either in the session or in the client's life outside) with the work that you are trying to do with him on his primary problem; second, if the secondary problem is the more important of the two from a clinical perspective;

and finally, if your client can see the sense of working on his secondary emotional problem first. Here you may need to present a plausible rationale to your client for starting with his secondary problem first. If, after you have presented your rationale, your client still wishes to work on his primary problem first, then do as he wishes. Otherwise, you may threaten the productive therapeutic alliance that you have by now established with your client.

In the case I am presenting, and as shown in Step 1, Bernie had ambivalent feelings about his anger. He saw that his anger led to negative results, but he also wondered whether bottling up his anger was a good alternative. However, Bernie disclosed no secondary emotional problems about his anger.

STEP 5: TEACH THE B-C CONNECTION

By now you will have assessed the A and C elements of your client's primary or secondary problem. The next step is to teach your client that his emotional problem is determined by his beliefs rather than by the activating event that you have already assessed. This is an important step. Unless your client understands that his emotional problem is determined by his beliefs, he will not understand why you are about to assess his beliefs in the next step of the treatment process. Spend some time on teaching the B-C connection if he has difficulty understanding it.

Therapist: Now do you think that everyone who is not doing well at work feels depressed about it?

Client: No.

Therapist: Why not?

Client: Well, people react differently to things.

Therapist: Right. Do you know why they react differently to the same event?

Client: People have different personalities?

Therapist: Well, that's a factor, but there's a more important reason. A famous Roman philosopher called Epictetus put his finger on it many years ago when he said "People are disturbed not by things but by their view of things." And psychologists today have done a lot of research which supports Epictetus' view. Namely that people make themselves psychologically dis-

turbed, including feeling depressed and angry,
by the attitudes they hold about events like not
doing well at work. Does this make sense?

Client: Yes I think so.

Therapist: Let me see, then, if I've made myself clear.
What's my point?

[I want to determine whether or not Bernie understands
my point so I ask him to put it into his own words. This
is an important strategy. RET therapists frequently have
to put points to their clients in a didactic manner, and it's
valuable to check whether or not clients understand what
they are being taught. To quote a well-known saying
"There is no good course without a test."]

Client: What you're saying is that I get angry because
of the attitude that I have.

Therapist: That's right. What do you think of that point?

[Not only do RET therapists want to ascertain that their
clients have understood their teachings, they also want to
find out their clients' opinions about these teachings.]

Client: Well it makes good sense to me.

Therapist: Well let's see how it relates to you personally.

STEP 6: ASSESS IRRATIONAL BELIEFS (iB)

You are now in a position to assess the irrational
beliefs that underpin your client's anger. You do this by
asking your client questions and giving him feedback with
respect to his answers. You continue this process until
you have correctly assessed his irrational beliefs both in
the form of a premise (e.g., dogmatic musts, absolute
shoulds, etc.) and the three main derivatives from the
premise (awfulizing, I-can't-stand-it-itis, and damnation).
There are two types of questions that you can ask
your client at this stage: open-ended questions and theory-driven questions (i.e., questions derived from rational-
emotive theory). An example of an open-ended question is
"What were you telling yourself about A to make yourself
angry?" A theory-driven version of the same question
might be "What *must* were you telling yourself about A to
make yourself angry?" Both types of questions have advantages and disadvantages.

The main advantage of the open-ended question is that it encourages your client to think more for himself in searching for the irrational belief that underpins his anger. The main disadvantage is that your client may well find it difficult to find the correct answer to your question, and may require a good deal of extra help from you. For example, in response to an open-ended question your client may well identify thoughts *other* than irrational beliefs (e.g., inferences) as "causing" his anger. If so, you will have to educate him otherwise.

The main advantage of a theory-driven question is that it quickly orients your client to look for his irrational beliefs. The main disadvantage is that you may be putting words into his mouth. If you encourage him to use his own words, however, this danger will be minimized.

Whatever type of question you use, one important task that you have during this stage of the assessment process is to help your client discriminate clearly between his irrational beliefs and his rational beliefs.

Therapist: First let's recap for a moment. We've agreed that the reason you made yourself angry about what you saw as Bill's provocative behavior was that it sort of touched a nerve in you, that is that you'd been feeling depressed about not doing too well at work. Bill's question seemed to remind you of something that you didn't want to be reminded of. Is that right?

Client: On the button.

Therapist: You also said that if you had been doing well or could handle not doing well in a more constructive way then you don't think you would have made yourself angry. Right?

Client: Right.

Therapist: So does it make sense to start with your feelings about not doing too well at work since that seems to be your view of your performance at work right now?

Client: Yes it does.

Therapist: OK. So you're feeling depressed about not doing too well at work and we know that your depression stems from an attitude. Let's see if we can't figure out together what that attitude is. What do you think you're telling yourself

about not doing too well at work to make yourself depressed?

[Note that I start with an open-ended question.]

Client: That I don't feel good about myself.
Therapist: Well let's see if you can be a bit more precise.
What belief do you have about yourself here to
make yourself depressed?

[Because Bernie has alluded to a derivative from an irrational premise, I start with that.]

Client: Well I guess I think I'm inadequate.
Therapist: An inadequate person?
Client: Right.
Therapist: That would lead you to make yourself depressed. But that view of yourself stems from
another belief. Let me explain. It seems important for you to do well at work. Right?
Client: Yes, sir.
Therapist: Well that's what we call a rational belief, and
if you stick to this belief you'd feel disap-
pointed about not doing well at work, but you
wouldn't feel depressed because your full version of that belief would be "I really want to
do well at work but there's no reason why I
have to do well."

[Note that once I've obtained one of Bernie's conclusions
from his irrational premise, I switch and try to identify
the irrational premise itself. I begin the process by intro-
ducing the idea of a rational belief so that I can encourage Bernie to identify his irrational belief through helping him to discriminate between the two.]

Client: Yeah, but I believe that I have to do well.
Therapist: And that's the point. If you escalate your rational belief to an irrational one, namely, I
absolutely have to do well at work, you'll be
depressed when you don't and you'll tend to
conclude "I'm inadequate when I don't do as
well as I must."
Client: Yeah, I can see that. I've never thought about
it that way before.

Therapist: Right. Also when you believe "I must do well at work" will you conclude that it's unfortunate but bearable when you don't?

Client: No. I'd believe that it's the end of the world and unbearable, which is exactly what I do think.

[Having helped Bernie to identify his irrational premise, I switch back to help him to identify his "awfulizing" and "I-can't-stand-it-itis" derivatives from that premise.]

Therapist: So let's recap and I'll write it up on the board so we can refer to it later. Your major irrational belief seems to be something like "I must do well at work," but why not put this into your own words.

Client: Er, "I must achieve good results at work."

Therapist: (Writing on the board) "I must achieve good results at work" OK, and since I'm not . . . let's recap. You said "I'm an inadequate person," "It's the end of the world," and "It's unbearable." Are those the right words?

Client: Yes.

Therapist: Right, but there's one more issue to deal with. Those beliefs that I've written on the board explain why you're depressed about not achieving good results at work, but they don't fully explain your anger at Bill. Given that you were vulnerable to being reminded of your own feelings of inadequacy, what must did you have about Bill's behavior to make yourself feel angry at him?

[I am now confident that we are dealing with self-worth anger in response to an inferred threat (see pages 13-14). In this type of anger it is important to assess and challenge *both* the irrational beliefs leading to self-worth depression and those that lead to anger at the source of the threat. Having assessed the former, I proceed to assess the latter. For the sake of brevity only the assessment of the irrational premise and one derivative from that premise will appear here. But first note that I have now used a theory-driven question to assess the irrational premise. I do this because Bernie has now some familiarity with the idea that *musts* lead to psychological problems.]

Client: He must not remind me of my inadequacy?
Therapist: Sounds that way to me. And what kind of person was he in your mind for doing what he must not?
Client: A rotten person. I could have killed him.

STEP 7: CONNECT iB AND C

After you have accurately assessed your client's irrational beliefs in the form of a premise as well as its derivatives, make sure that your client understands the connection between his irrational beliefs (iB) and his anger (or other disturbed emotions) at point C before going on to dispute these beliefs.

Therapist: Can you understand that as long as you demand that you must achieve good results at work and that you are an inadequate person if you don't then you are bound to make yourself depressed when you achieve poor results as you are currently doing?
Client: Yes I can.
Therapist: So in order to change your feeling of depression to one of disappointment, what do you need to change first?
Client: Why, that belief that I must achieve good results.
Therapist: That's right. And if you believe that other people must not remind you of your own inadequacy, can you see that this belief will lead to your angry feelings?
Client: Yes, and I need to change that belief as well.

In general it is more productive to elicit your client's understanding concerning the iB-C connection rather than telling him about it. If your client does not understand the connection between his irrational beliefs and his disturbed emotions, the "eliciting" approach is more likely to reveal this than the "telling" approach. It is worth devoting some time to helping your client to understand this connection before beginning to dispute his irrational beliefs. Otherwise, your client will not understand why you are challenging his beliefs.

STEP 8: DISPUTE iB

The major goal of disputing at this stage of the RET treatment sequence is to help your client to understand the following:

1. *Musts* - that there is no evidence in support of his absolute demands although evidence does exist for his preferences;
2. *Awfulizing* - that what he has defined as "awful" (i.e., 101% bad) is magical nonsense, and that in reality it will lie within a 0-99.9% scale of badness;
3. *I-can't-stand-it-itis* - that your client can always tolerate that which he thinks he cannot stand, and that he can be happy even if such negative events at A continue (although of course not as happy as he would be if those negative events did not exist); and
4. *Damnation* - (a) that all humans are humans, not devils or subhuman, and that they can be accepted as such even when they act badly; and (b) humans are fallible and too complex to be given a single global rating - a point which also applies to life conditions.

Don't expect your client to have achieved deep conviction in the rational alternatives to his irrational beliefs at the end of this step. The goal of this step is for you to help your client achieve intellectual understanding (or light conviction) of the point that his rational beliefs are more viable and more productive than his irrational beliefs. The goal of the subsequent steps is to help him deepen that light conviction.

When disputing your client's irrational beliefs you should endeavor to use open-ended, Socratic-type questions although you may need to use short, didactic explanations to clarify various points. When you ask a question, ensure that you get a correct answer to the question you have asked. If not, explain why the client's answer is incorrect and ask the question again in the same or modified form.

Keep in mind two points while disputing your client's irrational beliefs: (a) Use every opportunity to help him distinguish between his rational and irrational beliefs, and (b) don't switch needlessly from disputing an irrational premise to disputing an irrational conclusion. Keep on track.

Because of space constraints, in the verbatim excerpt that follows I will present the way I dispute some (but not all) of Bernie's irrational beliefs.

Therapist: Let's first look at the beliefs that lead to your depression and feelings of inadequacy, since they also increase your vulnerability to you making yourself angry. Now on the board we have "I must achieve good results at work." Let me ask you a question. We know that achieving good results is important to you, but where is the evidence that you *must* achieve what you want to achieve?

[Remember from the first section that irrationality has three major criteria: (a) It is empirically inconsistent with reality; (b) it is illogical; and (c) it leads to negative results. Thus I structure my disputing strategy according to these criteria in the above order.]

Client: Because I'd get on better if I do.
Therapist: That's why it would be better if you do well but note, Bernie, that I didn't ask you "Why would it be better for you to do well?", but "Why *must* you do what would be better?" Do you see the difference?
Client: Yes I think I do. Why must I do well? (Pause)
Therapist: Let me put it differently. If there was a law of the universe that said "Bernie must achieve good results at work" what would have to happen?
Client: I would do well.
Therapist: That's right. If that law existed in the world you would have no choice but to do well. But what's the reality?
Client: That I'm not doing well.
Therapist: Correct. So, in fact, you're demanding "What exists must not exist."
Client: That's silly.
Therapist: That's right. It's sensible to prefer to do well and to get good results because you can prove why you want to do well. For example, as you said, you would get on better if you do well. But it's nonsensical to demand that you must

	do well because you can't prove that you must and it goes against reality which is "You're not doing well."
Client:	So it's better to stick to my preferences and stop my demands.
Therapist:	Exactly, and for another reason as well. Is it good logic to say "Because I want to do well therefore I must?"
Client:	No of course not. It's bad logic.
Therapist:	Exactly. So that's a second reason to challenge your musts. But there's a third reason as well - a pragmatic one. Where's believing that you must do well going to get you apart from depressed?
Client:	Nowhere.
Therapist:	That's right. So there are three reasons to give up that must: (a) It doesn't reflect reality; (b) it's illogical; and (c) it will give you poor results, in this case depression.
Client:	Right. I'll just make a note of those reasons, I want to remember that.

[I will now present the disputing sequence that I carried out with Bernie with respect to his anger, namely the belief that Bill is a rotten person for reminding Bernie of his inadequacy.]

Therapist:	Now let's consider the belief that Bill is a rotten person for reminding you of your inadequacy. Let's suppose he does remind you of those feelings. Let's use our three guidelines to consider that belief. First of all is it consistent with reality to say that Bill is a rotten person?
Client:	No of course not.
Therapist:	Why not?
Client:	Because he's not rotten through and through, and even though he did a rotten thing like reminding me of my inadequacy I'm sure he didn't mean it.
Therapist:	Perhaps not but let's suppose he did mean it; he deliberately and maliciously set out to make you feel inadequate. Is he rotten for doing that rotten thing?

[Note that I discourage Bernie from reinterpreting Bill's intentions. I do so because I want to encourage Bernie to accept Bill as a fallible human being even if his "rotten" behavior was malicious.]

Client: No, I see what you mean. He's not rotten just because he's done something rotten.
Therapist: If he's not rotten what is he?
Client: Just human.
Therapist: Right. He's a fallible human being who has done the wrong thing. Now is it logical to say that he is rotten for doing a rotten thing?
Client: No, it's not.
Therapist: Because?
Client: It doesn't sound logical but I'm not sure why not.
Therapist: Well let's see. To say he has done a rotten thing means that you can isolate that one thing and say it was rotten. And remember we're assuming it is just for the time being. Does it make sense to say that he has done something rotten?
Client: Yes if he did deliberately try to make me feel bad then, yes, that was rotten.
Therapist: Right, but can we give Bill, who is a complex ever-changing human being, one rating which completely accounts for him in all his complexity, namely he is rotten just because he has done something rotten?
Client: No we can't. He's too complex for that, as you said.
Therapist: That's why it's illogical. It's illogical to evaluate the whole on the basis of a small part of the whole. Now let's see how pragmatic that belief is. Where is believing that Bill is rotten going to get you?
Client: Angry and we've already determined that anger will get me into trouble with Bill, my wife, and probably lots of others, too.
Therapist: So, again, use those three guidelines whenever you find yourself condemning someone as bad, rotten, or whatever.

I have chosen here to focus on one particular style of disputing irrational beliefs - that is, Socratic mixed with brief didactic explanations - because it is the style most favored and most often employed by RET therapists. For a more extended discussion of other styles of disputing, including the use of humor, therapist, self-disclosure, and vivid disputing methods, see Dryden, 1987; Walen, DiGiuseppe, and R. L. Wessler, 1980; and R. A. Wessler and R. L. Wessler, 1980.

STEP 9: PREPARE YOUR CLIENT TO DEEPEN HIS CONVICTION IN HIS RATIONAL BELIEFS

Once your client has acknowledged that (a) there is no evidence in support of his irrational beliefs, but there is evidence to support his rational beliefs; (b) it would be more logical for him to think rationally; and (c) his rational beliefs will lead him to more productive emotional results than his irrational beliefs, you may begin to help him deepen his conviction in his rational beliefs.

Point Out Why a Weak Conviction in Rational Beliefs Is Insufficient to Promote Change. Start by helping your client understand why a weak conviction in rational beliefs, although important, is insufficient to promote change. Do this by discussing briefly the rational-emotive view of therapeutic change. Using Socratic questioning and brief didactic explanations, help your client see that he will strengthen his conviction in his rational beliefs by disputing his irrational beliefs and replacing them with their rational alternatives within and between therapy sessions. Help you client understand that this process requires him to act against his irrational beliefs as well as disputing them cognitively. Establishing this now will help you later when you reach the stages of encouraging your client to put his new learning into practice (Step 10) and of facilitating the working-through process (Step 12).

Therapist: So you seem to understand now why your irrational beliefs are irrational and why the rational alternatives are more viable and will give you better results. But do you think this knowledge is all you'll need to overcome your anger and depression?

Client: I doubt it.

Therapist: Why?

Client: Because I've been thinking the way I do for a good while and it's going to take a while to change.

39

Therapist: Right. Imagine when you were young that you wanted to play golf and a kindly uncle offered to teach you. But the trouble was he taught you incorrectly. You practiced diligently those wrong strokes year after year but your handicap kept going up. Now imagine that I'm a golf pro and you came to me for help. I diagnose the problems with your stroke play, show you what you've been doing wrong, and show you how to play the strokes correctly. Now what will it take for you to internalize the new strokes?

Client: I'd have to practice the new strokes diligently.

Therapist: Right. Now what would your natural tendency be once you started practicing? Remember you've been playing incorrectly for years.

Client: Well the wrong strokes would feel natural and the new strokes would feel wrong.

Therapist: That's right, and you'd have to correct yourself once you caught yourself playing the wrong strokes and you'd have to persist with the correct strokes even though the wrong strokes felt right and the right strokes felt wrong. Now it's the same with the task ahead of you. On the issues we've been discussing, you've been practicing the wrong thinking strokes for years and in order to change them, you'll have to catch yourself thinking irrationally and correct yourself. Now you'll have to do that even though the new beliefs won't feel right for quite a while. You'll believe the rational belief intellectually but not emotionally, or as some people say "I understand it in my head but not in my gut." Now what do you think you'll need to do in order to get your new rational belief into your gut?

Client: Lots of practice.

Therapist: Right, and I'll be suggesting various assignments you can do to help you in that regard.

STEP 10: ENCOURAGE YOUR CLIENT TO PUT HIS NEW LEARNING INTO PRACTICE

At this point you can help your client choose from a wide variety of homework assignments that are advocated in RET. Before I list the major assignments that you can use with your angry clients, I will make a few general points about negotiating homework assignments.

Ensure That the Homework Assignment Is Relevant to Changing the Target Irrational Belief. Make sure that homework assignments are relevant to changing the irrational belief that has been targeted for change and that if the client carries out these assignments, he will be deepening his conviction in the rational alternative, that is, his rational belief.

Collaborate with Your Client. While you are discussing appropriate homework assignments with your client, enlist his active collaboration in the process. Ensure that he can see (a) that carrying out the homework assignment makes sense; (b) that if he does it, it will help him to achieve his goals; and (c) that he has some degree of confidence in his ability to carry out the assignment. Maximize the chances that your client will do the assignment by helping him to specify *when* he might do it, in *which* context, and *how frequently*.

Encourage Your Client to Carry Out an "Ideal" Homework Assignment but Be Prepared to Compromise. An "ideal" homework assignment will involve the client in actively disputing his irrational beliefs in a forceful manner and in the most relevant context. Try, if you can, to encourage your client to carry out an "ideal" assignment. If this is not possible, then encourage him to dispute his irrational beliefs in situations which approximate the most relevant A. You may find that if your client does these less "ideal" assignments, he may be more likely to carry out the "ideal" assignment later.

Assess and Trouble-Shoot Obstacles to Completion of Homework Assignments. While you are negotiating appropriate homework assignments with your client, encourage him to specify any obstacles that might prevent him from doing the assignment once he has agreed to do it. Encourage your client, if possible, to find ways of overcoming those obstacles in advance of carrying out the assignment.

I will now describe typical homework assignments that you can use with your angry clients. (For a fuller discussion of these and other homework assignments see Dryden, 1987; Ellis & Dryden, 1987; Grieger & Boyd, 1980,

Walen et al., 1980; and R. A. Wessler & R. L. Wessler, 1980.)

Cognitive Assignments

1. *DIBS (Disputing Irrational Beliefs)*. This is a formal version of disputing that includes some of its main components. An example that Bernie used is shown here:

Question 1: What irrational belief do I want to dispute and surrender?

Answer: Bill must not remind me of my inadequacy.

Question 2: Can I rationally support this belief?

Answer: No. I'd like him not to but it doesn't follow that he must not.

Question 3: What evidence exists of the truth of this belief?

Answer: None. If he reminds me of my inadequacy, then he should do so. If he reminds me of my inadequacy I can work on accepting myself with my poor performance at work.

Question 4: What evidence exists of the falseness of my belief that Bill must not remind me of my inadequacy?

Answer: Plenty. If he does, he should. The conditions are right. The conditions are that he asks me a question and I give myself feelings of inadequacy about the reminder that I'm not doing well at work. It's foolish to demand that this must happen.

Question 5: What are the worst possible things that could actually happen to me if Bill reminds me of my inadequacy?

Answer: Feelings of anger and inadequacy. These are unpleasant but hardly terrible.

Question 6: What good things could happen or could I make happen if Bill keeps on reminding me of my inadequacy?

Answer: I'd get plenty of practice at disputing my inferiority-creating beliefs.

DIBS is one example of cognitive homework that is frequently given to clients to do between sessions (see Ellis & Dryden, 1987, for other examples).

2. *Disputing on Tape.* Encourage your client to initiate and sustain a dialogue between the rational and irrational parts of himself. Ask your client to bring in the tape, and review it with him in the session, focusing particularly on irrational beliefs that he finds difficult to dispute.

3. *Rational Self-Statements.* Clients who find the process of disputing too intellectually demanding can be helped to develop rational self-statements which they can commit to memory or write on 3" X 5" cards and repeat at various times between sessions. These statements can also be used by clients who can engage in disputing at times when there is not sufficient time to carry out the entire disputing process. For example, Bernie developed the following rational self-statement which he repeated to himself at various times: "I'm a fallible human being who isn't doing as well as I'd like at work. Tough, but hardly awful."

4. *Rational Proselytizing.* In this assignment your client attempts to dispute the irrational beliefs of others that are similar to his own. In this way he gains practice at articulating rational arguments which he can then apply to himself. For example, Bernie successfully helped one of his friends to get over the latter's anger at his boss. He did so by showing his friend that although it was highly undesirable for his boss to frustrate his plans for promotion, there was no reason why his boss must not act in a frustrating manner.

5. *Rational Bibliotherapy and Audiotherapy.* In bibliotherapy, clients are given suggestions for self-help reading on the theme of anger (e.g., Ellis, 1977a; Hauck, 1974), and in audiotherapy clients can listen to audiotapes of their own therapy sessions as well as tapes of RET lectures on the theme of anger (e.g., Ellis, 1987a). These materials help clients to reinforce their new rational philosophy.

Emotive Assignments. The purpose of emotive assignments is a cognitive one - that is, to encourage your client to internalize his new rational philosophy. They more fully involve the client's emotions than do cognitive assignments.

1. *Rational-Emotive Imagery (REI).* In REI, your client gains practice at changing his feelings of anger to feelings of annoyance or displeasure while maintaining a vivid image of the negative event at A. This helps him learn to change his self-defeating anger by changing his underlying irrational beliefs.

> *Therapist:* OK Bernie, now close your eyes and vividly imagine that Bill is sneering at you and seeking to remind you of your own inadequacy. Now make yourself really angry about that and let me know after you've done that.
>
> *Client:* OK.
>
> *Therapist:* Now keep that same scene in your mind as vividly as you can but this time change your feeling of anger to one of displeasure and annoyance and let me know when you've done that.
>
> *Client:* (Pause) OK I've done it.
>
> *Therapist:* Now open your eyes and tell me how you changed your feeling from anger to annoyance and displeasure.
>
> *Client:* I told myself "Bill has a right to act this way, even though I don't like it." I also said "Just because he thinks I'm inadequate doesn't make me inadequate. I can accept my fallibility even if he can't."
>
> *Therapist:* Very good. Now I suggest that you practice doing that for 15 minutes, three times a day, until we next meet.

2. *Self-Dialogue and Self-Statements.* These assignments involve the same disputing methods and rational self-statements discussed earlier but carried out in a forceful and energetic manner. The purpose of these forceful assignments is to encourage the client to experience annoyance and displeasure while practicing his new rational philosophy.

3. *Shame-Attacking Exercises.* These exercises are particularly useful when your client's anger is based upon irrational beliefs leading to self-damnation. I encouraged Bernie to deliberately reveal to Bill the fact that he was not doing well at his job while attacking his shame by telling himself "I can accept myself with my poor performance even if Bill can't." When suggesting shame-attacking exercises to your client, caution him against acting in a way that would harm himself or others.

4. *Parables and Wise Sayings.* You can encourage your client to go over a number of parables and wise sayings that contain an anti-anger philosophy. Thus Bernie found the following saying very helpful in working on his anger problem: "Sir, I disagree with what you say, but I'll defend to the last your right to say it."

5. *Rational Humorous Songs.* Albert Ellis (1987b) has written a number of rational humorous songs that are designed to present rational philosophies in an amusing and memorable format. Often the message of these songs has its impact because it is delivered in a paradoxical way. One such song that Bernie found useful and sang to himself at relevant times is called "Pound, Pound, Pound" which is sung to the tune of "Jingle Bells" (words by Albert Ellis):

If you would get release
And let your anger out,
Disrupt the blasted peace
And scream and yell and shout,
Just go to any length
To show you can't be stilled
And you will show enormous strength -
Up to the time you're killed!

Pound, pound, pound! Pound, pound, pound!
Pound your enemies
Oh what fun it is to stun
Anyone who does not please you!
Sock, sock, sock! Knock, knock, knock!
Howl and whine and cry!
And everyone from you will run
And hate you 'til you die!

Behavioral Assignments. In behavioral assignments you encourage your client to take appropriate action and at the same time to challenge his irrational beliefs.

1. *"Stay in There" Activities.* These activities present angry clients with opportunities to tolerate frustration while remaining in uncomfortable situations for a long period of time. Such assignments are particularly useful for clients whose anger problems are based on a philosophy of low frustration tolerance. It is important that these clients practice a new philosophy of high frustration tolerance while they remain in the uncomfortable situation.

2. *Exposure to Criticism.* Clients whose anger is based on threats to their self-worth often strive to avoid other people who they believe are likely to criticize them. As a result they deprive themselves of the opportunity to accept themselves in the face of such criticism. "Exposure to criticism" assignments are designed to give clients such opportunities. Again it is important for clients to engage in appropriate cognitive disputing while they are exposing themselves to others' criticisms as Bernie did with Bill.

3. *Fixed Role Therapy* (Kelly, 1955). In RET, fixed role therapy is used to encourage clients to act "as if" they already think rationally, to enable them to get the experience of what it is like to act according to an anti-anger philosophy.

4. *Assertiveness Training.* Clients who have anger problems frequently do not assert themselves in an appropriate manner. They either communicate in an angry manner or say nothing at all about how they feel. In RET assertiveness training (see Lange & Jakubowski, 1976, for an extended discussion of a cognitive-behavioral approach to such training) clients are taught the skills of assertion together with an assertive philosophy based on respecting the rights of self and others and on accepting (but not liking) the fact that others may still act badly even after one has asserted oneself appropriately with them.

5. *The Use of Rewards and Penalties.* These are employed to encourage clients who have avoided undertaking uncomfortable assignments that are designed to help them practice their new philoso-

phy. Ellis (1985b) has found that stiff penalties are particularly helpful with chronically resistant clients.

Other Assignments. The 15 assignments that I have described are used to help clients adopt a new anti-anger philosophy based on rational beliefs. RET therapists do suggest that clients use other assignments which, though not designed to facilitate belief change, are helpful in other ways.

1. *Questioning the Validity of Inferences.* RET suggests that clients question the validity of their inferences under two conditions: (a) after they have achieved a measure of belief change, and (b) when, for a variety of reasons, they cling stubbornly to their irrational beliefs. As an example of the former, after Bernie had had some success at accepting himself for not doing well at work and at giving up his demands that Bill (and other people) must not remind him of his inferiority, I suggested that he question the validity of his inference that Bill was trying to show how great he was at Bernie's expense. In general, rational-emotive theory hypothesizes that clients will find it easier to question the validity of their negatively distorted inferences once they have achieved some measure of belief change. In my clinical experience I have found much evidence to support this hypothesis.

When clients cling to their irrational beliefs, you may be able to help them by getting them to question the validity of their inferences. You may help them temporarily overcome their anger by encouraging them to reinterpret the motives of others, for example. Thus, when clients infer that others have acted in an unfair, intentional, malicious manner, you could suggest that they collect evidence to test an alternative hypothesis, namely that the others were justified (from their point of view) in acting the way they did, that they accidentally committed the offense, and that there were good intentions behind their actions. This strategy, although helpful in the short term, does not generally lead to long-term productive results. As noted earlier, clients' irrational beliefs encourage them to make negatively distorted inferences, and if they

do not change these beliefs they will tend to continue to make such negative inferences in the future.
2. *Distraction Methods.* Helping clients to distract themselves from the frustrations, direct attacks, threats, and transgressions of life can be useful in helping clients to overcome their anger. It is particularly useful with clients who make themselves angry very quickly. Such methods as "counting to ten," the use of relaxation techniques, and the employment of "time out" procedures (where the client removes himself temporarily from the anger-provoking situation) are useful when they subsequently allow the client to challenge and change his irrational beliefs. When used on their own, these methods are palliative; although helpful in the short term, they have limited long-term therapeutic potential in facilitating belief change.
3. *Increasing Pleasures in Life.* Clients who have anger problems often have little pleasure in their lives. Helping them to increase their pleasures, particularly with others, is often a helpful adjunct to belief change methods. For example, clients who can gain greater pleasure in their relationships with others may become more able to forgive others when the latter act against the clients' interests.

STEP 11: CHECK HOMEWORK ASSIGNMENTS

Once you have negotiated a particular homework assignment with your client and he has undertaken to carry it out, check on what he learned from the experience at the beginning of the next therapy session. If you fail to do this, you show your client that you do not consider homework assignments to be an important ingredient in the process of change. Such assignments play a key role in helping your client to achieve his therapeutic goals. In particular, check that he actually faced the A that he committed himself to confront and that he changed the irrational belief that you both targeted for change.

If your client failed to execute the agreed homework assignment, accept him as a fallible human being for his failure and help him identify reasons why he did not carry out the assignment. In particular, use the ABC framework to encourage your client to focus on possible irrational beliefs that he held which served to prevent him from carrying out the homework assignment. Assess, in particular, whether or not your client held irrational beliefs indicating a philosophy of low frustration tolerance, for example, "It was too hard," "I couldn't be bothered," "I shouldn't have to work hard in therapy," and so on. If your client has such beliefs, encourage him to challenge and change them and then repeat the homework assignment.

If, however, your client failed to carry out the homework assignment because he lacked the necessary skills, help him acquire these skills before reassigning the task.

STEP 12: FACILITATE THE WORKING-THROUGH PROCESS

For your client to achieve enduring therapeutic change, he needs to challenge and change his irrational beliefs repeatedly and forcibly in relevant contexts at A. By doing so, your client will further strengthen his conviction in his rational beliefs and continue to weaken conviction in his irrational beliefs. This is known as the working-through process, the purpose of which is for your client to integrate his rational beliefs into his emotional and behavioral repertoire.

Suggest Different Homework Assignments to Change the Same Irrational Belief. When your client has achieved some success at disputing his irrational beliefs in relevant situations at A, suggest that he use different homework assignments to change the same belief. This serves both to teach your client that he can use a variety of methods to dispute his target irrational belief (as well as other irrational beliefs) and to sustain his interest in the change process. Bernie used a number of the 15 methods discussed previously to change his anger-creating and self-damnation beliefs.

Discuss the Nonlinear Model of Change. Explain that change is nonlinear and that your client will probably experience some difficulties in sustaining his success at disputing his irrational beliefs in a wide variety of contexts. Identify possible setbacks and help your client develop ways of handling these setbacks. In particular help your client identify and challenge the irrational beliefs that might underpin these relapses.

In addition, explain that change can be evaluated on three major dimensions: (a) frequency (does your client make himself disturbed less frequently than he did before?); (b) intensity (when your client makes himself disturbed, does he do so with less intensity than before?); and (c) duration (when your client makes himself disturbed, does he do so for shorter periods of time than before?). Encourage your client to keep records of his disturbed emotions at point C, using these three criteria of change.

At this point of the change process, encourage your client to read Albert Ellis' (1984b) pamphlet, *How to Maintain and Enhance Your Rational-Emotive Therapy Gains*. This contains many useful suggestions which your client can implement to facilitate his own working-through process.

Encourage Your Client to Become His Own Therapist. Encourage your client to develop his own homework assignments to change his target irrational belief and to experiment with changing his beliefs in different situations. After Bernie had achieved some success at disputing his irrational belief about poor performance when reminded about it in social situations, he began to dispute this belief at work. The more your client develops and carries out his own homework assignments, the more he will begin to serve as his own therapist. This is important because, as a rational-emotive therapist, your long-term goal is to encourage your client to internalize the RET model of change and to serve as his own therapist in the future after therapy has been completed. You know that you have been successful with a client when you have become redundant - which is exactly what happened to me with Bernie.

CONCLUSION

In this guide I have introduced some basic principles of rational-emotive theory and have focused on the rational-emotive approach to conceptualizing anger problems. Furthermore, I have presented and illustrated the rational-emotive treatment sequence as applied to anger therapy. While RET may appear simple, it is a difficult approach to master and I strongly recommend proper training for those new to RET. For further details about

RET training write to: Director of Training, Institute for Rational-Emotive Therapy, 45 East 65th Street, New York, NY 10021.

REFERENCES

Beck, A. T. (1976). *Cognitive Therapy and the Emotional Disorders.* New York: International Universities Press.

DiGiuseppe, R. (1988). Thinking what to feel. In W. Dryden & P. Trower (Eds.), *Developments in Rational-Emotive Therapy* (pp. 22-29). Milton Keynes: Open University Press.

Dryden, W. (1984). Rational-emotive therapy. In W. Dryden (Ed.), *Individual Therapy in Britain* (pp. 235-263). London: Harper Row.

Dryden, W. (1987). *Counselling Individuals: The Rational-Emotive Approach.* London: Taylor & Francis.

Ellis, A. (1962). *Reason and Emotion in Psychotherapy.* New York: Lyle Stuart.

Ellis, A. (1976). The biological basis of human irrationality. *Journal of Individual Psychology, 32,* 145-168.

Ellis, A. (1977a). *Anger--How to Live With and Without it.* Secaucus, NJ: Citadel Press.

Ellis, A. (1977b). The basic clinical theory of rational-emotive therapy. In A. Ellis & R. Grieger (Eds.), *Handbook of Rational-Emotive Therapy* (pp. 3-34). New York: Springer.

Ellis, A. (1980). Rational-emotive therapy and cognitive behavior therapy: Similarities and differences. *Cognitive Therapy and Research, 4,* 325-340.

Ellis, A. (1984a). The essence of RET - 1984. *Journal of Rational-Emotive Therapy, 2,* 19-25.

Ellis, A. (1984b). *How to Maintain and Enhance Your Rational-Emotive Therapy Gains.* New York: Institute for Rational-Emotive Therapy.

53

Ellis, A. (1985a). Expanding the ABC's of rational-emotive therapy. In M. J. Mahoney & A. Freeman (Eds.), *Cognition and Psychotherapy* (pp. 313-323). New York: Plenum.

Ellis, A. (1985b). *Overcoming Resistance: Rational-Emotive Therapy with Difficult Clients.* New York: Springer.

Ellis, A. (Speaker). (1987a). *How to Refuse to be Angry, Vindictive, and Unforgiving* (Cassette Recording). New York: Institute for Rational-Emotive Therapy.

Ellis, A. (1987b). The use of rational humorous songs in psychotherapy. In W. F. Fry, Jr. & W. A. Salameh (Eds.), *Handbook of Humor and Psychotherapy: Advances in the Clinical Use of Humor* (pp. 265-285). Sarasota, FL: Professional Resource Exchange.

Ellis, A., & Dryden, W. (1987). *The Practice of Rational-Emotive Therapy.* New York: Springer.

Grieger, R. (1982). Anger problems. In R. Grieger & I. Z. Grieger (Eds.), *Cognition and Emotional Disturbance* (pp. 46-75). New York: Human Sciences Press.

Grieger, R., & Boyd, J. (1980). *Rational-Emotive Therapy: A Skills-Based Approach.* New York: Van Nostrand Reinhold.

Hauck, P. A. (1974). *Overcoming Frustration and Anger.* Philadelphia: Westminster.

Howells, K. (1988). The management of angry aggression: A cognitive-behavioural approach. In W. Dryden & P. Trower (Eds.), *Developments in Cognitive Psychotherapy* (pp. 129-152). London: Sage.

Kelly, G. (1955). *The Psychology of Personal Constructs* (2 Vols.). New York: Norton.

Lange, A., & Jakubowski, P. (1976). *Responsible Assertive Behavior.* Champaign, IL: Research Press.

Moore, R. H. (1988). Inference as 'A' in rational-emotive therapy. In W. Dryden & P. Trower (Eds.), *Developments in Rational-Emotive Therapy* (pp. 3-11). Milton Keynes: Open University Press.

Tavris, C. (1982). *Anger: The Misunderstood Emotion.* New York: Simon and Schuster.

Walen, S. R., DiGiuseppe, R., & Wessler, R. L. (1980). *A Practitioner's Guide to Rational-Emotive Therapy.* New York: Oxford University Press.

Wessler, R. A., & Wessler, R. L. (1980). *The Principles and Practice of Rational-Emotive Therapy.* San Francisco: Jossey Bass.

If You Found This Book Useful . . .

You might want to know more about our other titles.

If you would like to receive our latest catalog, please return this form:

Name:_____

(Please Print)

Address:_____

Address:_____

City/State/Zip:_____

Telephone:(_____)_____

I am a:

_____ Psychologist   _____ Mental Health Counselor
_____ Psychiatrist   _____ Marriage and Family Therapist
_____ School Psychologist   _____ Not in Mental Health Field
_____ Clinical Social Worker   _____ Other:_____

◆   ◆   ◆

Professional Resource Press
P.O. Box 15560
Sarasota, FL 34277-1560

Telephone #813-366-7913
FAX #813-366-7971

Add A Colleague To Our Mailing List . . .

If you would like us to send our latest catalog to one of your colleagues, please return this form.

Name:_____
(Please Print)

Address:_____

Address:_____

City/State/Zip:_____

Telephone:(_____)_____

I am a:

_____ Psychologist   _____ Mental Health Counselor
_____ Psychiatrist   _____ Marriage and Family Therapist
_____ School Psychologist   _____ Not in Mental Health Field
_____ Clinical Social Worker   _____ Other:_____

◆   ◆   ◆

Professional Resource Press
P.O. Box 15560
Sarasota, FL 34277-1560

Telephone #813-366-7913
FAX #813-366-7971

*Would You Like Information On Our Other Publications?*_____

For a copy of our latest catalog, please write, call, or fax the following information to the address and phone number listed below:

Name_____
[Please Print]

Address_____

Address_____

City/State/Zip_____

Telephone_____

Profession (check all that apply):

_____	Psychologist	_____	Mental Health Counselor
_____	Marriage and Family Therapist	_____	Psychiatrist
_____	School Psychologist	_____	Not in Mental Health Field
_____	Clinical Social Worker	_____	Other:_____

Professional Resource Press
P.O. Box 15560
Sarasota, FL 34277-1560

Telephone # 813-366-7913
FAX # 813-366-7971

Add A Colleague To Our Mailing List . . .

If you would like us to send our latest catalog to one of your colleagues, please return this form.

Name:_____
(Please Print)

Address:_____

Address:_____

City/State/Zip:_____

Telephone:(_____)_____

I am a:

_____ Psychologist   _____ Mental Health Counselor
_____ Psychiatrist   _____ Marriage and Family Therapist
_____ School Psychologist   _____ Not in Mental Health Field
_____ Clinical Social Worker   _____ Other:_____

◆   ◆   ◆

Professional Resource Press
P.O. Box 15560
Sarasota, FL 34277-1560

Telephone #813-366-7913
FAX #813-366-7971

If You Found This Book Useful . . .

You might want to know more about our other titles.

If you would like to receive our latest catalog, please return this form:

Name:_____
(Please Print)

Address:_____

Address:_____

City/State/Zip:_____

Telephone:(_____)_____

I am a:

_____ Psychologist   _____ Mental Health Counselor
_____ Psychiatrist   _____ Marriage and Family Therapist
_____ School Psychologist   _____ Not in Mental Health Field
_____ Clinical Social Worker   _____ Other:_____

◆   ◆   ◆

Professional Resource Press
P.O. Box 15560
Sarasota, FL 34277-1560

Telephone #813-366-7913
FAX #813-366-7971